T0249152

LOVE POEMS

(for Anxious People)

LOVE POEMS

(for Anxious People)

JOHN KENNEY

G. P. Putnam's Sons / New York

PUTNAM
— EST. 1838 —

G. P. PUTNAM's SONS
Publishers Since 1838
An imprint of Penguin Random House LLC
penguinrandomhouse.com

Copyright © 2020 by John Kenney
Penguin supports copyright. Copyright fuels creativity, encourages diverse voices, promotes free speech, and creates a vibrant culture. Thank you for buying an authorized edition of this book and for complying with copyright laws by not reproducing, scanning, or distributing any part of it in any form without permission. You are supporting writers and allowing Penguin to continue to publish books for every reader.

Cataloging-in-Publication Data is available from the Library of Congress.

ISBN 9780593190685
ebook ISBN 9780593190692

Printed in the United States of America
3rd Printing

To . . .

There are so many people I should dedicate this book to.

But I can't seem to pick one.

What if I make the wrong choice?

Or offend someone?

This is a nightmare.

My life has been full of terrible misfortunes
most of which never happened.

MICHEL DE MONTAIGNE

LOVE POEMS

(for Anxious People)

AUTHOR'S NOTE

What follows is a work of fiction.

I have almost no personal experience with feelings of anxiety.

Unless you include puberty, college, my twenties, and most any sexual encounter I have ever had.

Thank you.

What to think if someone has given you this book as a gift

Perhaps you are thinking, *Hey. Someone has just given me this book and it has the word* anxious *in the title. Asshole.*

Don't worry. Just because someone gave you this book does *not* mean they think you are anxious or uptight or have "issues."

But chances are you are anxious and uptight and most likely have issues. And no, that is not an insult. It is a compliment. It means you are very likely an interesting person.

But also complicated and probably difficult to live with, even though you think you are easy to live with (a classic sign of someone who is difficult to live with).

The point is to simply enjoy the book in the spirit with which it was given. Which most likely was a ploy to get you to see a therapist. Also to possibly regift it to a person you know who, like you, has serious emotional issues.

What to think if you bought this book for yourself

Good for you.

It says a great deal about you that you would carry around a book with the word *anxious* in the title. Especially since you are not anxious.

Oh sure, there's a little bubble of fear that sits in your stomach most days. But who doesn't have that? (Calm people.)

Anxiety is a total stranger to you. Well, maybe not a total stranger. Maybe you see anxiety in the neighborhood from time to time. Heck, maybe you have welcomed anxiety into your home, had a coffee and a laugh. Well, maybe not a laugh so much as a question. And that question was about your persistent cough and whether you should have an MRI that very day.

The point is to relax. Remember, you are not an anxious person. And you are holding a book with the word *anxious* on the cover to prove it.

But also thinking that maybe you should return it and hoping you've kept the receipt.

**What to think if you borrowed this book from
a friend or the library**

Really?

You couldn't buy this?

I'm a freelance poet, for God's sake.

Do you have any idea how hard it is to get the IRS to
even recognize that as a real thing?

Wow.

WebMD

It started out simple enough.
A brief search.
Kanker sore.
Which I spelled wrong
and now realize is a district in India
as well as the Dutch slang
for a very bad word
and also, somehow, cancer.
Which led me to a site that linked
canker sores to cold sores
showing how oral cancer lesions
can mimic an open canker sore,
symptoms of which include
mouth pain and difficulty swallowing
(both of which I suddenly had)
as I followed a link to
the definition of head and neck cancer
which I did not know was a thing

nor did I realize I was now at risk of it
as a result of my mouth lesion/canker/cancer sore
which often causes
golf-ball-size tumors
resulting in blindness, lack of motor function,
and complete sexual dysfunction.
Which is good to know.
Then I looked up an earache I was having
and it turns out I have two months to live
or possibly a head cold.

Eulogy

We are here today
to celebrate the life
of Martin Greengrass
father, grandfather, dear friend.
And I, Nathan, his eldest grandson,
have been chosen—
honored, really—
to give his eulogy.
Where do I begin?
Boy was he old.
Also, apparently *eulogy* is from
the Greek word "to praise."
Or possibly "to die."
I'm not sure, as I just looked that one up
on my phone.
If I appear a bit nervous
it's because I am.
The thing is

I have never given a eulogy.
But I wrote something last night
and put it on my desk
next to the work presentation
I have later tomorrow
to our agency's Coffee Mate client.
And so what I have here
is, in fact, my Coffee Mate presentation.
The irony, of course, is that Martin loved Coffee Mate.
The original flavor
but also French vanilla, Irish crème,
and our newest flavor,
hazelnut.
I would now like to open it up for questions
about Martin
as well as Coffee Mate's marketing strategy for Q4.

Here comes someone whose name I should know

We have met so many times
you and I.
And yet I have no idea
what your name is
as I stand
frozen
inane grin on my face.
Do you have a name?
Here you come
smiling
calling my name
as well as the names of my wife
children
and dog, Fortinbras.
Which I kind of can't believe you remember.
My God, you're almost here.
And I will need to introduce you
to the person next to me

whose name may be Beth. Or Valentina. I'm not sure.
Here's a quick thought.
Not about your name
but about the urge I have right now
to just start running.
That would be a weird thing to do, though,
at a children's birthday party.
But not as weird as what I do.
Which is stuff two cupcakes
into my mouth
so as not to be able to speak
but almost immediately choke
spewing frosting
on your face.
Ohmigod, Alan, Beth/Valentina shouts.
Alan.
His name is Alan.
Which I will now never forget.

Am I meditating yet?

Am I doing this right
sitting here
cross-legged
trying to empty my mind
or clear my mind
or not think
or just be.
I forget which.
The thoughts aren't real
according to the voice
on the meditation app.
They're just clouds floating by.
Wait. Does that mean it's going to rain?
Whoops.
Watch them go by.
Soft, floating clouds.
Smile at the clouds.
Fake smile. Sadness.

Whoops.

Breathe.

Be.

Be late for work.

Get fired.

Never work again.

Become homeless and die on the streets in your own filth.

Or balloons, the voice says.

Thoughts are like balloons.

Gently pop the thought.

But if you pop a balloon

the sound is very loud and makes children cry.

I hate that sound.

Will I ever have children?

Sometimes I am impotent in the bedroom.

Deep breath.

Day one, completed.

Honest date

Kate?

Yes. Hi. Adam?

Yeah. Hey.

Hey.

Wow. So.

I don't know how to start a conversation.

You have beautiful breasts.

Do you want a drink?

A beer would be great.

*I'm having beer, too. Ha. You're shorter than I imagined. So
    nervous.*

Ha. Are you laughing at me? I hate my own face. Have
    you been here before?

*To this bar? No. Nope. So Tina tells me you're in
    marketing? Do you like that?*

I hate it. But I'm too afraid to leave because I have no
    self-esteem. You?

I'm not really sure what my company does. Sometimes at work I just sit in the stall in the ladies' room and cry.

My penis is small and shaped weird and looks like a baby turtle. I heard it's supposed to snow later. I like snow.

I love snow. I hate sex though. So . . . That's a nice watch.

Thanks. It was incredibly expensive and I regretted buying it almost immediately. I bought it to feel love I never received from my mother. But it is water resistant.

I hate my sister so much.

Want to share an appetizer? I use masturbation to avoid anxiety.

Sure. I'm going to stay seated, though, because I'd like to punch my thighs in the face, if that makes sense.

Okay. Did I mention I'm terrified of public bathrooms?

This is so much worse than I thought it would be. Tequila?

Sounds good.

A friend hasn't texted me back yet and I am totally fine with that

It's fine. She's busy. Who isn't busy?
It's just that it's been a few days
and it was an awesome picture
of my appetizer
at a restaurant.
Whatever.
Weird though.
She could have at least hearted it.
I mean, it's a nice photo if you like arugula (which she
     does).
It's fine. Is it though?
Two days. Nothing. Well, a day and a half, technically.
And she definitely saw it.
Read. The text said *Read.*
So I know she read it.
And then ignored it.
Or laughed.

Laughed at my photo of my appetizer which,
sure, appeared to just be arugula, but it also had beets
  and shaved Parmesan.
And now I'm an asshole.
Maybe this nice-person façade was total crap.
I should have trusted my gut when I initially liked her
but then wondered if she was too nice.
She's a horrible person.
And I should tell her that.
Wait.
A text from her. Finally.
So hey. My grandmother died.
That would explain things.
Still. Commenting on my salad would have killed her?

Incredibly relaxed at the beach with the kids

Look at me
    relaxed
at the beach
    with the kids
slathered in sunscreen
    as I sit huddled under an umbrella
large hat
    and T-shirt
hiding all skin from the sun
    which I am enjoying
but also deeply aware of its cancer-causing rays.
    The ocean looks lovely
but also deadly.
    Riptides jellyfish sharks
German submarines.
    Well. Not for some time now. But still.
Get away from the water! I scream at the children
    without realizing I was going to scream.

This is so much fun. The beach.

Sand in my sandwich.

I have forgotten my sunglasses

and my retinas feel like they are melting.

Traffic home will be bad.

I saw a T-shirt once.

Life's a beach. And then you die.

It might have said life's a bitch. Not beach.

I have bad vision.

Which, come to think of it, could also be glaucoma.

Old friends

I am having a party
at home
alone
and so many of my old friends are here.
Anxiety, look at you sweating.
Say hello to my good friend Embarrassment.
I think you both met in junior high.
And over here by himself
facing the wall
is my friend Shame.
And there
unaware
that his fly is down
and cream cheese is on his face
is my dear friend
Awkward Moment.
And what a treat!
Self-loathing just walked in.

I haven't seen you since I looked in the mirror this
     morning.
And you brought Regret.
I wish you hadn't.
That was a joke.

Job interview thank-you note

Thank you again
for taking the time
to meet with me this morning.
And also respecting my schedule
by cutting our thirty-minute interview
to just seven minutes.
I am glad you were able to see
in that remarkably short window
how much I would love the opportunity
to work for your company.
I would also like to apologize
again
for complimenting the photo
of your grandmother
on your desk.
I did not realize that she was
in fact
your wife.

I should add that I often laugh
when I am nervous
which was why I was laughing
as I was escorted from the building.
I look forward to hearing from you.

My condolences (and a few other thoughts)

I am so sorry for your loss
I said to the family members
when I finally made it
to the front of the line.
And I was.
I was also sorry
that the line was so long
which I also mentioned
by mistake.
How it had been, like,
forty-five minutes and my legs
were killing me.
I should not have used the phrase *killing me.*
But the casket was open
and I was sure I saw something move
and was briefly startled
in the way seeing a ghost can startle you.
Or make you almost wet yourself.

The problem was I mentioned that too.
Also that I almost wet myself (which I may have a bit)
because I thought I saw the body moving.
(Turns out it didn't.)
In fairness
they had already been crying a bit
before I got to the front of the line.
Though perhaps not quite so loudly.

Have a nice day

At school drop-off
one of the moms called out
casually
"Have a nice day!"
And I thought
What the hell did she mean by that?
Does she think I don't have nice days?
Was she being sarcastic?
Does she not think I'm nice?
She kind of hit the word *day*
as if to say
Have a nice day, you freak.
Did I say something wrong?
Why did she use the word *nice?*
Does she think my days aren't normally nice?
Maybe it was the *have.*
Have a nice day.
What does that even mean?

Like I don't have any purpose to my days?
I'll tell you what I have now.
I have a headache and a pit in my stomach
thanks to that bomb you just dropped on me.
So thanks for that.
You have a nice day too!
That's what I should have said.

Teacher's note home about the upcoming second-grade field trip

We are *so* excited about the upcoming field trip.

A few gentle reminders.

The bus will leave promptly at 8:20am.

Children arriving later than 8:20am will not be allowed
    on the bus.

It is imperative that no one brings *anything* that has nuts.

I'm not kidding. Don't do it. I swear to God.

This includes anything with the *word* nuts

even if it is a child's stuffy named "Peanut."

(That stuffy has been confiscated.)

Also eggs or any egg product or anything made with
    eggs or egg-shaped toys.

No dairy.

Nothing with sugar or sugar substitutes.

No store-bought fruit.

There will be no plastic on the bus.

This includes plastic bags, plastic water bottles, plastic toys.

There will be no speaking on the bus.

Children who speak on the bus will be removed from the bus and left by the side of the road.

The trip to the museum is approximately twenty minutes in length.

Due to liability, at no point will the children be allowed *in* the museum.

They can look at the museum from a distance of no closer than one hundred feet.

No photos or drawings.

Any child who sings will be punished.

Thank you and we are so excited!

Today is going to be a great day

I know that because
that's what my daily affirmation app says.
Ping!
Today is going to be a great day, Helen!
It knows my name
and uses exclamation points
which annoy me a little.
So far, though,
today has kind of sucked.
Yesterday my affirmation said
I love and accept myself!
Which, I have to admit, did not pan out.
(I didn't and I don't.)
The day before that was
I can handle anything life throws at me.
Well, that's true.
If the line had continued
    . . . by crying and curling into a ball under my desk at work.

I have some ideas for daily affirmations.

I will wet myself a bit when a car tailgates me and leans on the horn, surprising me.

Or

If you see someone you know and they haven't seen you, hiding behind a bush is perfectly acceptable behavior.

Or

Like yourself a little bit, but also kind of beat the hell out of yourself for that asinine comment you made to your boss.

I e-mailed my ideas to the app.

But I have yet to hear back.

In conversation with myself (2:49am)

I'd like to go back to sleep now.

Oh, I don't think quite yet. We have things to talk about.

I don't want to talk. I want to sleep.

Or we could play a fun game.

Or sleep.

Nope. Fun game time.

What's the game?

It's called "Your life is a complete failure."

That's not a fun game.

It is for me.

But aren't you me?

Yes and no.

And can't I control you?

Good luck with that. Let's review your twenties.

Please don't.

*You poured a pitcher of beer on your head at a happy hour
     with your boss present.*

Oh Christ.

Then you . . .

Nope . . .

*C'mon. I love this one. You said, "Look at the rack on that
waitress."*

I didn't know she was his wife.

*What about that time, in a meeting, you thought Arkansas
ended with the letter "w" . . .*

You suck.

*And wrote it on a whiteboard in a staff meeting and
everyone laughed. At you.*

I'm going to sleep.

Fine. Good night.

Really?

Sure. Sleep well.

Oh. Okay.

Lyme disease.

What?

Nothing . . .

I have thrown a can of Coke in the trash and not the recycling bin

I wasn't thinking.

I just threw it away.

And then saw the face of the woman standing on the
    subway platform.

A disgusted look.

As if to say, you disgust me

for your lack of concern about the environment.

And also maybe because I was drinking a Coke

which is bad for me.

Why was I drinking a Coke?

I'm such an asshole.

I felt bad.

I threw the can away wrong.

So I went to get it out.

But a homeless man reached for the can ahead of me.

And I smiled and said I wanted it back

to throw away in a recycling bin.

He refused and then told me to do a quite rude thing to
    myself.
I tried to explain about the environment and 2 degrees
    Celsius
and how the world was coming to an end.
He said that wasn't his problem and that he was just
    trying to buy more booze.
Someone must have called the police
because the next thing I knew I was explaining the can
and the environment and the guilt thing
to police officers
who did not seem as receptive to
my plight as I had hoped.
To this day I have no idea where the can went.
And that bothers me.

Do you find my anxiety sexy?

When I question whether the chicken might be too old to
    cook,
is that a turn-on for you?

When you're driving and I say be careful in case a deer
    jumps into the road
(which admittedly rarely happens in Brooklyn),
do you find yourself in the mood?

When I overreact because the front burner was left on
    and could burn the house down,
even though it's electric and was on low,
is the look you're giving me a signal to get nude?

I didn't think so.

Where are you going?

Honey?

Okay then.

Just . . . be careful.

Teaching a five-year-old how to cross the street

We wait for the walking-man sign,
I tell my son
at the intersection.
See how now
it's red and it says Don't Walk?
We don't walk.
In fact, we don't even move.
Unless it's to move back
away from the street.
Farther, so that your back is against the wall of this
    building.
See that jackass on the bicycle?
He's too close to us.
Isn't jackass *a bad word?* you ask.
Not in this case.
It says Walk now, Mom.
But that's exactly when you shouldn't walk.
Not yet anyway.

Look both ways.

Now look again.

Now look a third time.

What do you see?

Nothing.

Well you're not looking hard enough.

Even when it says you can walk

you can't walk.

Can you tell Mommy why?

Because some asshole from Jersey could blow through the light?

Good boy.

Our weekend without the kids

Alone
finally
in the car
just us two.
A night away at the fancy hotel.
Should we call them
you said
on the drive, smiling
but also serious.
Nope, I said. *We shouldn't.*
Your parents are fine with the kids.
You're right, you said.
This is so fun without them.
When we got to our room you said,
Is it weird that I miss them?
I thought it was incredibly weird
as I barely remembered their names at that point.
I wanted to drink an overpriced beer

and have sex.
You had other fun plans.
Those plans included sitting
at the foot of the bed
with a glass of wine
crying
while looking at pictures of the kids on your phone.
So sex is probably off the table, I said
as we checked out an hour later.
I think the man at the front desk thought I was talking
    to him.

Unanswered e-mails to my editor (part 1)

Dear Sally,
Struggling a bit with the "anxious" book.
Isn't that funny? I'm anxious writing it.
Ha ha.
Seriously though, I feel like I'm dying.
I'm also a little drunk.
Which is funny, too.
Here's a thought.
Maybe we change the title.
Love Poems (for People Who Cry for No Reason).
I could write that one. Kidding. Sort of.
Write back soon.
Haven't heard from you in a while.

John (Kenney)
(I'm one of your authors)

P.S.

I know that I am contractually obligated to deliver by
    January 30.

But that's a crazy time frame . . . Maybe you were joking?
    (Hope so!)

John

Unanswered e-mails to my editor (part 2)

Hey Sally,

Are you on vacation?

I have some new ideas instead of the book about anxious
people.

Is that a good idea to maybe change it up?

My therapist says it is.

Also that I should be on 100 mg. of Lexapro, not 5.
Seems like a big jump, right?

Love Poems (for Insects). Because who doesn't love
insects?

Love Poems (for People Who Love Clowns).

*Love Poems (for People with Exceptionally Low Self-
Esteem).*

Love Poems (for Middle-Aged Men with Many Regrets).

*Love Poems (for People Who Find a Deep Sadness in the
Everyday).*

*Love Poems (for People Who Don't Like the Company of
Other People).*

*Love Poems (for People Who Are Known by Their First
    Name at the Local Wine Shop).*

*Love Poems (for People Who Have Tripped and Fallen
    upon Walking into a Meeting Wherein They Had to
    Present Something and Who Then Said, "Fuck Me!" and
    Who Then Regretted That Reaction).*

I like a lot of these if you do.

E-mail soon.

Also, I could use more time! Not kidding!

John

Unanswered e-mails to my editor (part 3)

Hey Sally,

Seriously though.

You don't mean January 30 of this year, right?

E-mail anytime.

Quick question.

Are you still technically my editor?

Because a lot of these e-mails are bouncing back.

Thanks.

John

Tipping

I ordered a latte to go
at the hipster coffee shop
in my new neighborhood
smiling at the thought
that I would soon be a regular there.

Hey Stan, this same bearded barista
will surely say
in the days to come.

The usual, dude?

He'll nod and smile like
All good, man
and I'll nod and smile even though
I don't want the usual. I want tea.

But I've already nodded.

No matter.
We will probably become friends
and maybe he will tell me why he thought
it was a good idea
to get a tattoo of a question mark on each earlobe.

Feeling the budding relationship inside me
I placed a tip inside the jar
sure he would see my largesse
perhaps nod and smile
as if to say
You're the man, bro.
(Which I'm normally not.)

But my soon-to-be good friend
turned away
before seeing me tip
which was disappointing
as it was a five-dollar bill.

So what I did was
reach back in to get it
so I could do it again
when he was looking.

But as I reached in
he turned to ask
if I wanted soy or whole milk.

Here's something else about the new neighborhood.
Not three blocks away
there is a Dunkin' Donuts.

What I should not have said to my new boss on the phone

I will grant you
that it was late in the day
and I was driving
and had you on speaker
listening to your instructions
for the next day's meeting.
I'm still new
and you are intimidating
but also kind of dull
so I was spacing out a bit.
And maybe I did drift
to thinking about how good
a cold beer at home would be
taking off most of my clothes
sitting on my ass on the couch
looking for a new job
as I kind of hate this one already.

And then it was time to hang up.
And you said,
I'll see you at 7.
And I said,
Okay. Love you.
I didn't mean to say that.

In conversation with myself (3:31am)

Tell me your worst fears.

Please be quiet.

Tell me.

No.

*How can a grown man be afraid of water bugs? That's
    just . . .*

Move on.

You have the beard of a fourteen-year-old boy.

That's not my fault.

Ovinophobia.

That's an actual thing!

*Fear of sheep? Really? I bet a lot of the guys at D-Day had
    that.*

It doesn't make me less of a man.

Yes, it does.

Yeah, it does.

C'mon. What else. You know I love this stuff. Worst fears.

Dying in my sleep.

That's funny. And incredibly common. What else?

It's not common.

Say the other thing. I love the sound of it.

No.

Say it.

You suck. Frisbees.

Dying in your sleep and Frisbees. Wow are you a mess. God,
    I would hate to be you.

Small talk in an elevator

I miss yesterday's weather
I said, innocently enough
to the woman in the elevator at work.
You missed it? Where were you?
No, I said. *I miss it.*
Miss what? she asked, annoyed.
The warm temperatures. Amazing for this time of year.
Yeah. But it was freaky for January.
Absolutely. I didn't mean I was glad about global warming.
  Just that it was nice. Like spring.
Spring in January? It's like an eco-Holocaust.
I certainly didn't mean to suggest that.
Two more degrees Celsius and the world comes to an
  end.
Totally. Plus, I have weekend plans. I'm kidding, I was
  just . . .
The whole Celsius thing confuses me.

Oh. Just multiply the temperature in Celsius by two then
     multiply it by one-fifth and subtract the result from
     step two from the number in step one. Then add
     thirty-two.

Seems like a lot.

Really? To figure out the future of the planet?

No, I certainly didn't mean that. Just the math part . . .

And then, noticing her bump, I said,

So when are you due?

I shouldn't have said that.

She's not due.

You can really get a sense if someone is not pregnant

by the look they give you

as they get off the elevator.

"Make of yourself a light,"
said the Buddha,
before he died.

—from "The Buddha's Last Instruction," by Mary Oliver

**The Buddha's second-to-last instructions
(with apologies to Mary Oliver)**

"Make of yourself a light,"
said the Buddha,
before he died.

Before that, though, he said some other things.

He said, "You guys, I've been sitting so long I think my
    leg is asleep." Then he laughed and it was awkward
    because no one else laughed.

He said, "It's so hot here. Is anyone else incredibly hot? This heat is horrible."

A couple of people nodded.

He said, "Sometimes I get nervous for no reason. Does that ever happen to you?"

Two people nodded, rolled their eyes, and said, "Totally."

He said, "Remember when I said the 'life is suffering' thing? I was in a really bad mood, super-anxious about this woman I know and this project I was working on that was a nightmare. Anyway. I didn't mean it."

He said, "About the heat thing from earlier. Did I say that out loud or think it?"

And one of the people watching him said, "You said it out loud." But the person said it in a way that was kind of obnoxious. His name was Greg.

The Buddha kind of looked at him like, whatever.

He said, "I would kill for ice. Not literally, but you know what I mean. Don't be a dick and take me literally, Greg."

That shut Greg up.

Then he said the thing about the light. But no one really
   knew what he meant.
Whereas with the heat and ice thing, it was like, yeah, we
   get it.

Why is everyone staring at me?

Do I have something on my face?

Toilet paper on my shoe?

Have I tucked my shirttail
into my underpants by mistake
and people can now see my underpants?

Because I feel like people
are staring at me.

Sure, some are looking at their phones
and others are yawning.

And, granted,
I am giving

a presentation
in a conference room.

But still.

Stop staring at me.

To the man on his phone at 7-Eleven who bumped into me and spilled iced coffee on my pants and said, "Whoops," and then walked away

You seemed nervous
blinking a lot
shoulders at your ears.
In a world that too often lacks
empathy
I empathized with you,
new friend.
Glued to your phone
as if it were the face of God.
(Turns out it was TikTok.)
Also, don't worry about me.
I'm fine.
Who needs an apology?
Or a napkin, for that matter,
when simply walking away
still staring at your phone

will suffice.

And no, I don't really hope you get hit by a bus
or fall down an elevator shaft.

That was just a reaction.

But I do hope you need your wallet today.

Because you dropped it.

And I have it.

Whoops, indeed.

A review of the conversation I just had

It's a good thing people aren't like that
I hadn't meant to say
to the beautiful woman
at the dog park.
It just sort of popped out.
Sorry, what's that?
she said, smiling.
And here I could have said any number of normal things.
But I panicked.
And what I said was
You know . . . just . . . like . . . going up to each other . . .
(I was sure I wouldn't say it. But I did.)
sniffing each other's . . .
(Again, I had the chance to stop but I didn't seem to be in
control of my mouth.)
sniffing each other's butts.
Then I added
against my will

Imagine. Just walking up and . . .
Yup, she said.
I wanted to tell her
I hadn't meant to say any of that.
That it had come out wrong.
That no one dislikes me more than me.
But that maybe we could still grab a drink sometime.
But she was gone by then.

Train of thought

When the subway stops
the world stops
a bit.
The wait to see
if it will ever start up again.
The train, that is.
And when the lights and air-conditioning go out
I wonder if I have left the iron on
until I remember that I don't own an iron
but that I do have borderline high cholesterol.
A silent killer, my doctor said.
It's a marvelous name, I said.
Boom. Dead. Guess who's laughing then?
(I guess he meant he would be laughing?)
Also suffocation.
A thing that can happen in tunnels
deep under the East River
where the train sits now.

Why doesn't the weight of the river crush the tunnel
drowning everyone?
(Well done, tunnel builders.)
How many rats are there down here?
The Wi-Fi still works.
Wow.
Anywhere from 250,000 to tens of millions of rats live in
New York's subway tunnels.
Death by rat.
Is that a thing?
Also sociopaths.
One in one hundred people in America is a sociopath.
Surely there are more than one hundred people in this
very packed car.
Would you rather die by rat or sociopath?
Which I hadn't meant to say out loud.
But I do now have a bit more room around me.

Ode to *All Things Considered*

Oh, Ari Shapiro.
And here I thought we were friends.
I have some news for you.
Do you know what's not news to me?
The news.
See what I did there?
You are no fun anymore
you bearer of relentless awfulness.
Hurricane, flood, tsunami.
Glaciers and global and warming.
Polls and partisans and politics.
Do you think those stories make me feel good?
(They don't.)
I don't feel well at all, Ari.
My doctor has advised me to stop all news intake.
I don't think you folks consider all things.
Just bad things.
Maybe consider some other things.

Like donuts. Or kites. Or vodka.

Vodka is nice to consider.

Do three hours on vodka.

(God knows I have and it's not even noon.)

Live from NPR News in Washington, I'm Ari Shapiro. And this is All Vodka Considered.

Next night is whiskey. Then Wellbutrin.

Help me, Ari.

You and Nina and Lakshmi and Audie and that other guy whose name no one knows.

I don't feel well.

No one does.

Be my Tom Cruise to your Cuba Gooding Jr.

Help me, help you.

Consider it?

To my therapist of nine years

I came to you
so many years ago
an anxious, confused mess.
(Your words.)
And now look at me.
An anxious, confused, older mess.
(Also your words,
after which you chuckled.)

You said you would help me overcome my obstacles
no matter where I was on my *journey toward change.*
I remember thinking that the phrase
journey toward change
was amazing.

Now I wonder if we were both drunk when you said it.

You said we could *integrate my mind with my body.*

That was interesting to me
but also kind of freaked me out.

And no, I don't think we are making progress.
Unless progress means going backward.
Maybe you have a saying about progress going backward?
I don't suppose you offer any kind of money-back
    guarantee?

In conversation with myself, 4:12am

Stop.

You can't stop thinking, Brian.

My name isn't Brian.

I know. But I like to annoy you.

I can stop thinking.

No. You can't.

I can. I'm doing the Headspace app with the soothing
   Englishman. I signed up.

Really, Greg . . .

My name's not . . .

How many sessions have you done?

A few.

Two. You've done two. And checked e-mail both times.

God you suck.

Rude.

I'm rude?! You won't shut up.

Do you want me to shut up?

Of course.
Okay. I'm shutting up.

Yeah right.

Really?

Wait. Am I controlling my own mind?

This is amazing.
I was kidding. I'm still here. Let's play the profound regrets loop, yeah?
Sounds like a plan.

Sit back, relax, and enjoy the flight

Looking back
it was probably a mistake
when the flight attendant asked me
if I wanted something to drink
to ask her if she knew
how much the plane weighed.

It's certainly not what I had wanted to say.
I had wanted to say "tomato juice."

And when I started to ask if she might have a wedge of
    lemon
I happened to say that a Boeing 737 weighs 175,000
    pounds.
So why doesn't it just fall from the sky?

Also peanuts, if you have them
I had meant to say.

But instead said

The skin of a Boeing 737 is just three-quarters of an inch thick.

She had stopped scooping the ice for my drink by then.
And when I pointed to the can and asked if I could have the whole thing
what I said instead was
It's a wonder it doesn't just implode like a can of tomato juice.

I have no recollection of saying
Death happens in the sky!
but apparently eyewitnesses corroborate it.

I never did get that tomato juice.
But I did get to sit next to the air marshall.

Nice to meet you

Now what do I do?
With my hand, I mean.
The one you just shook
with your germ-infested one.
Are you a clean man?
You don't look it to me.
Sure, you are a senior client
in charge of marketing.
But where has that senior client hand been?
Not under scalding water like my hand.
And now you have ruined that.
You have been talking since we shook hands
though I do not know
for sure
what you have been saying
as I have been thinking
about my dirty hand.

I was just going to grab a sandwich.
But I can't now.
I have to go back to the bathroom.
When I said *Nice to meet you*
earlier
I was lying.

Was I a dick to the waiter?

I sighed.
That was the problem.
I mean, it was no big deal.
Fine, I sighed with a little attitude.
I may have also made a face
when he said they didn't have the IPA I like.
I also may have mumbled the word
Seriously?
There was that little frozen moment in time
when the waiter and my wife were thinking precisely the
    same thing.
What a dick.
I knew it, too, of course.
I didn't need the look from my wife.
The one that says
I wish I hadn't married you
because you were a dick to the waiter.
Their looks have pushed me over

the cliffs of regret and shame,
and I am falling now
loathing myself even more than normal.
Thinking things like
Maybe I don't deserve to live
and *Why didn't I just order a vodka tonic?*

I will go to a party alone

Look at me.

I'm dressed.

I'm dressed in nice clothes and I've showered.

It's Saturday night.

I'm wearing cologne that smells powerfully of pine trees.

But there is only so long

a person alone

can stare at his phone

in the lobby.

I am not nervous.

I'm a grown man, for Chrissakes.

In a large city.

I'll get in that elevator and go up to that party.

Hey, I'll say to the host and his wife.

Great party.

Although maybe I shouldn't say that right away

as I would have just gotten there and that would sound
    dumb.

Maybe I'll say *I don't know what kind of party this is yet*
and laugh.

Heck, maybe I'll say *This party sucks.*

But they might think I was being rude.

Where's your liquor? I could say.

I want to drink your liquor, I could say in a funny voice.

And then wink.

Do people wink?

I could also go back to my apartment.

Imagine this poem is funnier than it is

How funny would that be
if this were really funny.
Imagine yourself laughing right now.
Ha ha ha.
Tears streaming down your face.
Not because you're sad
but because you're crying with laughter
at how funny *this* poem is.
Seriously.
And you know what the thing is
that's making you laugh so hard?
A really funny notion about anxiety,
which, if you think about it,
isn't funny at all.
But this poem is so good that it *makes* it funny.
(Which is hard to do!)
And the best part would be
a surprisingly funny ending.

(That's the hardest!)
And then what you'd have
is a really funny poem.

**For my brother, Tom. The least anxious person
I ever knew.**

Your mustache was ridiculous.
You knew that, right?
Long, drooping handlebars
falling below your chin.
A kind of Wild West cowboy
quiet confidence to match.

You knew who you were
from the age of five.
A firefighter
like our father and both grandfathers.
Like them you were made different
calm in a world so afraid.

What's it like in a burning building
I asked you once.
Warm, you said.

But it came out *wahhm*
thick Boston accent
a little sideways glance
Irish twinkle
living for a laugh in the face of pain.

I think fear was afraid of you.
Anxiety too anxious to touch you.
You were too tall too strong too sure.

How proud Mum would have been of you.
Just five foot one
she would stand
on a kitchen chair
to comb your hair before school.

We were in the same room
your room
when dad told us
she was dead.
I was looking out the window,
twelve years old to your twenty.
How does that not connect two people forever?

You were Bud Light and Ford Ranger
Stanley tools and a cigar by the grill

Steely Dan and the James Montgomery Band
the Doobie Brothers and Duke and the Drivers.

You were the one
in the news photos
after the rescue
covered in soot
fire coat open
out of breath
a child in one arm
and a Halligan in the other
looking at the camera
as if daring it to challenge you.

The Book of Isaiah says,
And I heard the voice of the Lord saying, Whom shall I send?
Then I said, Here am I. Send me.

Send me, you said.
So He did.
And then He took you
too soon
like Mum.

I'm not afraid, you told me.
I know you weren't.

There is a
space
now
in the cadence in my head
the one I have known
since I learned how to speak
the
one
Mum
stumbled through
to get to one of our names.

CharlieMichael Tom PatJohnTim.

Here's what you thought of anxiety and fear.
The last time I saw you
you were sitting in a chair
covered with a blanket
too thin now
waiting
for the other brothers to arrive.
A final visit.
We heard their car pull into the driveway.
You looked at me
eyes wide
that little twinkle

then slumped down in the chair
dropped an arm over the edge
and whispered,
Hey.
Tell them they're too late.
A tiny smile
crossing your dry lips
as you closed your eyes.

ACKNOWLEDGMENTS

Thank you to the good people at G. P. Putnam's Sons, especially Sally Kim, Ivan Held, Gaby Mongelli, Ashley Hewlett, Alexis Welby, Ashley McClay, Emily Mlynek, and Katie McKee.

Trusted readers and idea generators: Robin Kall and Emily Homonoff. Josephine Sittenfeld and Thad Russell. Zibby Owens, Anna Toumey, Alexa Englander, Klodet Torosian, Lynnette Blanche, Lauren Sachs, Louise Dougherty, Rick Knief, Gabrielle Obermeier, and Amanda Close.

To my children, whose names escape me at this moment. Wait. Lulu and Hewitt.

And to my wife, Lissa, surely one of the least anxious people I have ever met. She edited every line in this book, made my bad ideas good. And suggested I see my therapist five times a week, not just one.

ABOUT THE AUTHOR

John Kenney is the *New York Times*–bestselling author of the poetry collections *Love Poems for Married People* and *Love Poems for People with Children*, and the novels *Talk to Me* and *Truth in Advertising*, which won the Thurber Prize for American Humor. He has worked for many years as a copywriter. Kenney has also been a contributor to *The New Yorker* since 1999. He lives in Brooklyn, New York.